Mr. Noisy's Book of Patterns

When Mr. Noisy talks, he goes:

2

When Mr. Noisy walks, he goes:

Click Click Clack! Click click Clack!

3

When Mr. Noisy sings, he goes:

When Mr. Noisy dances, he goes:

Tip Tap Tap Tap!
Tip Tap Tap Tap!
Tip Tap Tap Tap!

Tip Tap Tap Tap!
Tip Tap Tap Tap!
Tip Tap Tap Tap!

5

When Mr. Noisy drives his car, he goes:

Zoom Rattle Bang
Zoom Rattle Bang
Zoom Rattle Bang

When Mr. Noisy rides his bike, he goes:

And when Mr. Noisy sleeps, he goes: